EXPLORER TRAVEL

MOUNTAINS

Chris Oxlade

Chicago, Illinois

© 2014 Raintree
an imprint of Capstone Global Library, LLC
Chicago, Illinois

To contact Capstone Global Library please phone 800-747-4992,
or visit our web site www.capstonepub.com

Edited by Adam Miller, Laura Knowles, and Claire Throp
Designed by Steve Mead
Original illustrations © Capstone Global Library Ltd 2014
Illustrated by H L Studios
Picture research by Tracy Cummins
Production by Victoria Fitzgerald
Originated by Capstone Global Library Ltd
Printed in China by China Translation and Printing Services

17 16 15 14 13
10 9 8 7 6 5 4 3 2 1

Library of Congress Cataloging-in-Publication Data
Oxlade, Chris.
  Mountains / Chris Oxlade.—1st ed.
    p. cm.—(Explorer travel guides)
  Includes bibliographical references and index.
  ISBN 978-1-4109-5430-5 (hb)—ISBN 978-1-4109-5437-4 (pb) 1.
Mountains—Juvenile literature. I. Title.
  GB512.O9 2013
  910.914'3—dc23   2012042362

Acknowledgments
We would like to thank the following for permission to reproduce
photographs: Alamy p. 31 (© Max Stuart); Corbis p. 28 (© HO/
Reuters); Getty Images pp. 8 (Jonathan P. Ellgen), 14 (Stephen
Collector), 23 (Andrea Solero/AFP), 26 (John Terence Turner),
36 (Eddie Kosmicki/Bloomberg), 37 (Shaun Curry/AFP); Hugh
Tuffen p. 12 (© Hugh Tuffen); Neil Champion pp. 5 middle, 34
(© Neil Champion); Shutterstock pp. 4 (© Microstock Man), 5
bottom, 33 (© My Good Images), 5 top, 10 (© Peter Wey), 6
(© cozyta), 15 (© Isabella Pfenninger), 16 (© Lutsan Pavlo), 17
(© Dennis Donohue), 19 (© Narongsak N.), 20, 38 (© Petunyia),
21 (© Lee Prince), 22 (© Martin Lehmann), 39 (© Galyna
Andrushko); Superstock pp. 18 (© Wolfgang Kaehler), 25
(© Prisma), 27 (© Henry Georgi/All Canada Photos), 32
(© William Stevenson).

Design elements: Shutterstock (© pchais), (© Nik Merkulov),
(© vovan), (© SmileStudio), (© Petrov Stanislav Eduardovich),
(© Nataliia Natykach), (© Phecsone).

Cover photograph of Cerro Torre seen from Agostini camp,
Los Glaciares National Park, Patagonian Andes, Argentina,
reproduced with permission of Getty Images (Colin Monteath/
Hedgehog House).

We would like to thank Daniel Block for his invaluable help in the
preparation of this book.

CONTENTS

Some words are shown in bold, **like this**. You can find out what they mean by looking in the glossary.

Don't forget

These boxes will give you handy tips and remind you what to take on your mountain adventures.

Amazing facts

Check out these boxes for amazing mountain facts and figures.

Who's who

Find out more about mountain experts and explorers of the past.

Conservation

Learn about conservation issues relating to mountains.

WELCOME TO THE MOUNTAINS!

You have chosen to explore some of the world's most amazing places! Sights to see in the mountains include towering, rocky, and snow-capped **summits**, vertical cliffs, icy **glaciers**, deep gorges, tumbling streams and rivers, and spectacular views. The mountain peaks themselves are not the only sights. A wide variety of plants and animals live on their slopes. Also, there are the villages and towns of the people who live and work in the mountains.

The great peaks of the Himalayas are the highest of the world's mountain ranges.

What is a mountain?

A mountain is simply a place where the landscape rises steeply above the lower, flatter land around it. There is no rule to say when a hill is high enough to be a mountain. In some countries, a hill about 3,000 feet (1,000 meters) above sea level is thought of as a mountain; in other places, this would just be a small **foothill**.

Most of the world's mountains are part of **mountain ranges**. A mountain range is an area where there are many mountains in a group or a long line. Enormous mountain ranges include the Himalayas, in Asia; the Andes, in South America; the Rockies, in North America; and the Alps, in Europe. In total, mountains cover about one-quarter of the world's land (not ocean) surface. Many **volcanoes** are also thought of as mountains.

Amazing facts

The Himalayas contain the highest mountains in the world on land, including the highest of all, Everest, at 29,035 feet (8,850 meters). The Andes is the longest range, at around 4,500 miles (more than 7,000 kilometers) from north to south.

TURN THE PAGE...

Find out about erosion on page 11.

Meet a real-life mountain explorer on pages 34-35.

Learn more about avalanches on page 33.

BEFORE YOU GO

Knowing how mountains are made, what physical features they have, and what the weather is like will help you decide which mountain you would like to visit first.

Mountain types

Mountains are built up in two ways: they are either pushed up by the movement of rocks in Earth's **crust**, or they are built up by volcanic activity. There are three main types of mountains that are built up by the movement of rocks: fold mountains, block mountains, and dome mountains (see the diagram on page 7).

These layers of rock have been folded into mountains by immense forces.

These mountain-building processes take thousands or millions of years. The Himalayas are quite young mountains, but they still began to form more than 600,000 years ago. Since Earth was formed about 4.5 billion years ago, many mountain ranges have been built up and worn away. So, you have missed the chance to explore them!

Bumping plates

Earth's crust is a solid, rocky skin that covers the planet. It is cracked into many giant pieces, known as **tectonic plates**. The plates move very slowly, and in some places their edges push into each other or one plate slides under the other. This movement pushes up fold mountains. But sometimes the rocks do not bend to form mountains. Instead, they crack (or fault) and form block mountains.

 Who's who

Alfred Wegener (1880–1930) was a German scientist who realized that the coastlines of South America and Africa fit together like two pieces of a jigsaw puzzle. He suggested that Earth's continents are slowly moving, and that about 250 million years ago all the continents were joined together in one giant continent, which he called Pangaea, meaning "all the Earth."

The three types of mountain

Fold mountain

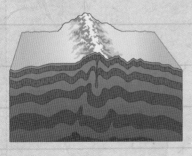

Rocks push together at edges of tectonic plates

Block mountain

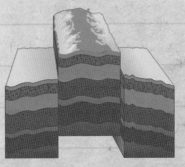

Huge block of rock rises or falls

Dome mountain

Molten rock rising from under Earth's crust pushes upward

Volcanic mountains

A volcano is a place where molten rock (called **magma**) from under Earth's crust makes its way to the surface. The magma solidifies, forming new rock. Over time, the new rock builds up to form a mountain.

Most volcanoes erupt along the edges of tectonic plates, where one plate slides under another. Rock in the lower of the two plates gets very hot and melts, and the magma forces its way to the surface. Volcanoes also form at places called hot spots in Earth's crust, where magma from below pushes upward. The islands of Hawaii are the tops of volcanoes that have grown over a hot spot on the floor of the Pacific Ocean.

Traveling by cable car allows people to see an amazing view of Mount Fuji, in Japan.

Types of volcano

There are several different types of volcano, but the two types that build up the highest mountains are stratovolcanoes and shield volcanoes. Stratovolcanoes erupt **ash** and thick **lava**, which build up into steep-sided, cone-shaped mountains. Shield volcanoes erupt runny lava. This flows down the volcano's slopes and solidifies, building up a mountain with gently sloping sides.

So, which mountains would you like to visit? The high, icy peaks of a fold mountain range or the crater of a fiery volcano?

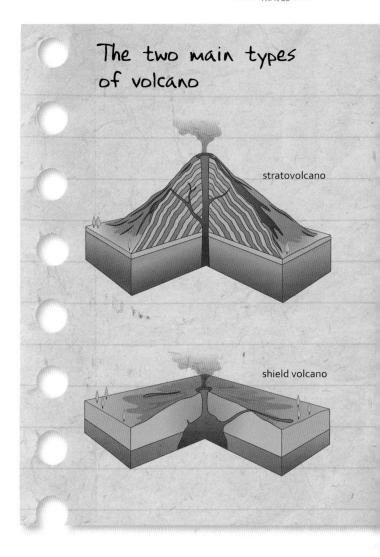

The two main types of volcano

stratovolcano

shield volcano

Don't forget

All mountain exploring can be dangerous, but **active volcanoes** have extra hazards! Hazards include red-hot lava, poisonous gases coming from the ground, and **pyroclastic flows**, which are avalanches of roasting-hot ash. You will need some special equipment such as sturdy boots to protect your feet from hot, sharp rocks on volcanoes. If you are going near lava flows, you will need to borrow a heat-reflecting suit. This is covered with metal foil so that the heat from the lava bounces off it.

Mountain climate

The big thing you will notice about exploring mountains is the weather! The **climate** on mountains is generally colder, wetter, and windier than it is on the plains below the mountains. The atmosphere is colder higher up, because it is not warmed as much by heat from Earth's surface. It is windier because air has to flow up, over, and around mountains, and it gets squeezed as it does so, which makes winds stronger. It is wetter because rain clouds form if moist air rises to pass over mountains. The air cools as it rises, and water vapor in it turns to liquid water, which makes clouds and rain. Cold temperatures also mean that snow falls on mountains when it is raining on the plains below.

These jagged peaks have been made as the weather has cracked and broken their rock.

Weathering and erosion

The harsh weather breaks up the rocks that mountains are made of. This process is called weathering. When water freezes in cracks in rock, it can split the rock apart, and particles of rock blown along in strong winds knock pieces off rocks. Other rocks may dissolve or become soft in water. The loose pieces of rock fall down the mountainside, are washed away by water, or are blown away. Gradually, mountains are worn away. This process is known as **erosion**.

Amazing facts

Mountain ranges can create deserts. They force air upward, which makes the air cool, clouds form, and rain fall. By the time the air reaches the far side of the mountains, there is no rain left to fall. The land here is very dry, and the area is known as rain shadow. The Tibetan Plateau is a very dry area in the rain shadow of the Himalayas.

The physical features of mountains

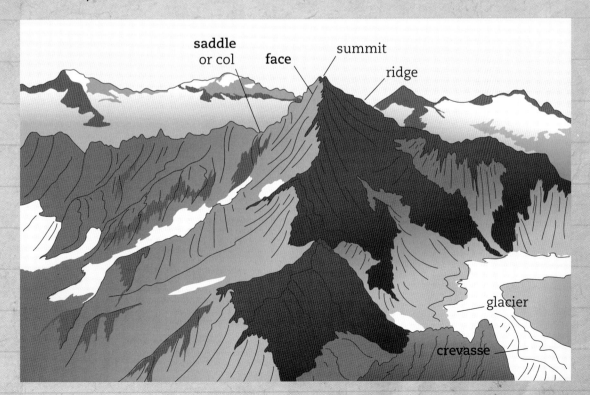

INTERVIEW WITH A VOLCANOLOGIST

Dr. Hugh Tuffen is a volcanologist and a college professor.

Q: What do you do in your job as a volcanologist?

A: I get to visit both active and **extinct** volcanoes in exciting countries such as Iceland, Chile, and Japan. This is to watch volcanic eruptions and to collect samples of lava and **pumice** formed in past eruptions.

Q: When did you become interested in volcanoes?

A: When I was seven, I got a book about volcanoes and kept on reading it again and again. I loved looking at the pictures of lava rising up from under the ground and making new mountains. I found out that some mountains [near where I live] are actually extinct volcanoes that erupted a long time ago. I started to dream that they were active again and I had to climb them to rescue people who were trapped in the ash!

Q: Is there anything in particular that you enjoy about volcanoes or visiting volcanoes?

A: I love visiting volcanoes because they are exciting, wild places that are formed in dramatic eruptions. I love climbing volcanoes, seeing the spectacular views, thinking about how the earth under our feet is alive, and then bathing in a hot spring!

Q: Have you ever seen a volcano erupting?

A: I have been lucky to see several volcanoes erupting. The most memorable one was Puyehue Cordon-Caulle in Chile. We camped close to the crater as explosions sent a plume of ash high into the sky above us and sent out huge booming noises that kept us awake all night. In the morning, our tents were covered in ash.

Q: Do you have a favorite volcano?

A: My favorite volcano is Torfajökull in Iceland. I've been lucky to spend many months there and have gotten to know the volcano very well. It last erupted in 1477.

Q: Are there any volcanoes that you would particularly like to visit?

A: I would love to visit Mt. Erebus in Antarctica. I'd like to see its boiling lava lake, its deep crater, and the ice caves made by heat from the crater.

Q: What hazard of visiting volcanoes scares you the most?

A: I am most scared of pyroclastic flows. When camping on the side of an active volcano, I always avoid valleys, as pyroclastic flows tend to travel down them. It is much safer to stay on higher ground.

DISCOVERING NATURE

Huge numbers of plants and animals live in the world's mountain ranges. The plants and animals are **adapted** to the harsh conditions, and some even survive on the snowy, rocky mountain summits. These distinct communities of plants and animals are known as **biomes**.

Plant zones

Imagine climbing from the bottom of a mountain to its summit. You might walk through **coniferous** forests on the lower slopes. Then you will find **alpine** meadows. Eventually, you would reach a height where no plants can grow, known as the summit zone. These different levels of a mountain are known as plant zones. They exist because of the different climate at different levels of a mountain. The main zones are **deciduous**, coniferous, alpine, **tundra**, and summit.

Lush green forests grow on mountain slopes in Peru.

Small plants come into flower when snow melts in spring in alpine meadows.

Plant adaptations

Mountain plants are adapted to life at high **altitude**. For example, alpine flowers can grow where there is very little soil. Their roots grow into cracks in the rocks, allowing them to hang on in strong winds. They also grow low to the ground, to avoid being damaged by the wind.

 # Who's who

Joseph Hooker (1817–1911) was a British botanist (person who studies plants). He went on many scientific expeditions around the world to study plants. He visited the Himalayas, the Rockies, and the Atlas Mountains in North Africa, discovering many new **species** of plants and collecting thousands of samples to take back to the Royal Botanic Gardens in London, England, where he worked.

Fur coats

Mountain animals have thick coats to insulate their bodies from the cold, and the coats get thicker as winter approaches. The yak, which lives in the Himalayas, has two layers of fur: a dense layer of short hair, with long, shaggy fur on top. The snow leopard has fur on the bottom of its paws, and it can wrap its furry tail around itself like a blanket.

Sure-footed ibex search for food on the steep, rocky slopes of the Alps.

 ## Don't forget

Mountain animals are tricky to get close to. Often they can walk on steep slopes that are hard and dangerous for humans to get to. Smaller animals hide quickly under rocks if you get too close! Make sure you take a pair of binoculars or a small telescope, so you can get a good look at them from a distance. You could also take a guide book about animal shapes and footprints to help you identify the animals.

Living at altitude

High in the mountains, the air is thinner than it is lower down. This means there is less oxygen for animals to breathe. Llamas live high in the Andes. They have large lungs and also have more red blood cells in their blood than any other mammal. Lungs transfer oxygen from the air into red blood cells, and the cells carry it to where it is needed in the body.

Surviving winter

In winter, it is hard for animals to find food in the mountains. Some animals move to lower altitudes, where the weather is less harsh. Other animals **hibernate** instead. For example, the marmot, which lives on mountains throughout Europe, Asia, and western North America, hibernates for about six months in a burrow under the alpine meadows where it lives.

Predators, such as the mountain lion, hunt over a large area because food is scarce. Only a few mountain lions could survive in a range of 30 square miles (78 square kilometers).

MOUNTAIN LIFE

Rocks, snow and ice, plants, and wildlife are not the only things you will see when you explore mountains. You will also meet the people who have made the mountains their home because there are good pastures for animals, space to live, and beautiful surroundings. Farmers living on the slopes of volcanoes grow crops in the rich volcanic soil.

Adapting to the mountains

Reasons for living in mountains differ between poorer and wealthier nations. Many tribes of people have lived in the mountains for hundreds and even thousands of years. Over time, they have learned the skills needed to survive, such as how to keep warm and grow crops. Like mountain animals, people who live at high altitudes have become adapted to the thin air.

The **indigenous** people of Ecuador have more red blood cells to carry oxygen around their bodies than average humans.

Machu Picchu

The spectacular mountain settlement of Machu Picchu in Peru was built about 550 years ago by the Inca people. The Incas built here because the mountains were a natural protection against invaders. People who live in the mountains around Machu Picchu today live in a similar way to the Incas, growing crops and raising animals.

Machu Picchu stands 7,972 feet (2,430 meters) up in the Andes.

 Conservation

In some mountain areas, such as the country of Nepal, people have cut down forests, mainly for firewood. Nepal lost a quarter of its forest between 1990 and 2010 alone. With the trees gone, the soil is washed away, and floods and landslides are more common. Today, people are trying to prevent illegal **deforestation** and to introduce alternatives to wood for fuel, such as solar power. In many areas, mountain forests are now managed by governments to balance use, conservation, and recreation.

Working in the mountains

Most of the people who live in the remote mountain areas of Asia and South America are small-scale farmers or herders. They grow crops for themselves, to barter or to sell at local markets, or they raise animals such as llamas and yaks to trade. Some people live as **nomads**, moving from place to place to find new pastures for their animals.

Animal helpers

Herd animals are important for mountain people. In the Andes, people have raised llamas for thousands of years as **pack animals**, for carrying goods. People use the llamas' wool to make clothing, rugs, and even ropes, use their hides to make clothes, use their dung as fuel for fires, and eat their meat. In the Himalayas and Tibetan Plateau, people raise yaks, which are large animals like cows. The yaks provide milk, butter, and meat and are used as pack animals—and even for yak racing!

Farmers build terraces on steep mountain slopes to create flat fields for growing crops.

Growing crops

When you visit many mountainous areas of the world, you will see long, narrow fields on mountain sides. These are called terraces. They make space for farmers to grow crops such as rice, corn, and potatoes on steep slopes. They also help to stop soil from being washed away in heavy rain.

Conservation

The world's mountains are important resources for forestry and energy and for leisure. But in many places, local people are ignored by the mining, forestry, and energy industries that take the resources. In the past, people have even been forced from their land, but today, many mountain areas are protected, and local people control which industries are allowed to operate.

Copper ore is dug out at the Bingham Canyon Mine in the mountains of Utah. The mine is one of the biggest human-made holes in the world!

Early explorations

Every good explorer should know about the adventurous people who first set out into the mountains. The world's mountain ranges are like barriers to travel. Thousands of years ago, people faced long and treacherous journeys if they wanted to cross mountains to find new places to live or to trade goods. There were no roads, maps, or modern clothing. In ancient times, armies sometimes lost thousands of troops to the cold as they crossed mountain ranges to explore and conquer other countries.

Today, you can take road or rail tunnels under some mountain ranges, such as the Alps, but in most places, you still have to go over mountain **passes** to get from one side to the other.

Roads and railroads have opened the way for everyone to travel in the mountains.

Scaling the peaks

In the 19th century, explorers started to climb mountains just for the challenge of getting to the top. They started in the Alps, climbing peaks such as Mont Blanc and the Eiger. Today, mountaineers climb in all the world's mountain ranges. In 1953, Tenzing Norgay and Edmund Hillary became the first climbers to reach the summit of the world's highest mountain, Mount Everest.

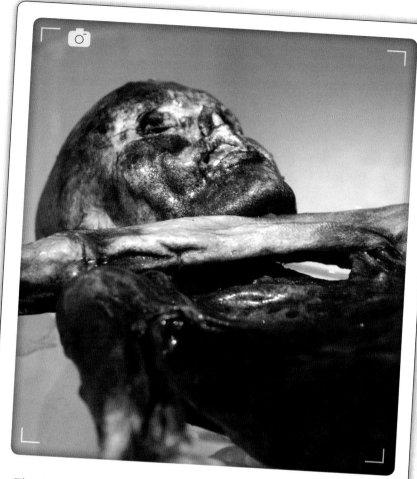

This body was found preserved in ice high in the Alps. It is 5,300 years old and shows that people crossed over mountains in the distant past.

 # Who's who

Reinhold Messner (born 1944) is an Italian mountain climber who achieved many mountaineering firsts. In 1978, he became one of the first two people to climb Mount Everest without using oxygen to breathe. In 1980, he climbed Everest again, but this time solo. Later, he became the first mountaineer to reach the top of all 14 mountains in the world that are taller than 8,000 meters, or about 26,250 feet.

PLANNING YOUR TRIP

There are lots of things to decide before you set off to explore the mountains. First, you will need to choose which mountains to visit. Read some guide books and study some maps to help you decide. Now you can decide when to go, how to travel, what equipment to bring, and whom to take with you.

When to go

When you travel to the mountains depends on what sort of exploring and what kind of activities you want to do. Traveling around in the mountains is easier in the summer, when snow and ice melt away and mountain passes are open. But you will need to go in the winter if you want to do winter sports, such as skiing. You might want to visit an active volcano. The best places to go include the Big Island of Hawaii and Stromboli, in Italy, where volcanoes erupt nearly all the time.

 Conservation

Exploring mountains can often cause environmental problems. Try to be responsible as you explore. For example, never leave any trash behind, stay on paths and trails to reduce erosion, don't camp in one place for more than a few days, and don't cut wood for fuel. You should also follow local customs, so that you don't upset local people.

Amazing facts

When Mount St. Helens volcano in Washington state began to erupt in 1980, thousands of people flocked to the area because they wanted to see an eruption for themselves. Many visitors ignored police road blocks to get close to the action. They thought they were still a safe distance away, but there was a giant explosion and a pyroclastic flow swept over the landscape. Fifty-seven people were killed when they were buried by the hot ash.

In the summer, you can travel over high mountain passes on local buses.

What to wear

Mountain clothes must keep out rain, wind, and cold. That means you should wear a base layer for warmth and to take sweat away from your skin, a middle layer for warmth, and a waterproof outer layer. When it is warm and wet, you need a "breathable" outer layer of clothes, which keeps out rain but lets sweat escape.

You need strong boots, with good grip, for walking on steep, rocky ground. For snow and ice, you will need something called crampons on your boots, which have metal spikes underneath. Trekking poles, like thin walking sticks, will help you climb steep mountain slopes.

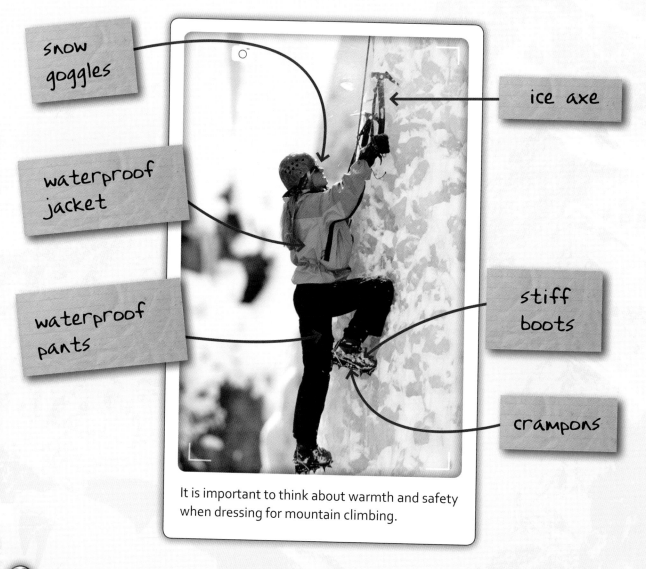

snow goggles

ice axe

waterproof jacket

waterproof pants

stiff boots

crampons

It is important to think about warmth and safety when dressing for mountain climbing.

More equipment

For long trips, you may need a tent or other form of shelter, a sleeping bag, a stove, and other camping equipment. But make sure it is lightweight, because you will have to carry it in a backpack. You will also need to bring water or a way to make the water you find along the way safe to drink. Take some equipment for navigation, including maps, a compass, and a **GPS receiver**.

You will also need an expert to show you the way and to teach you how to use climbing equipment such as ropes and harnesses. You might also need a few tanks of oxygen if there is a danger of **altitude sickness**.

Don't forget

Snow reflects sunlight very well, and if you look at it for too long, your eyes could be damaged, making them swell. This is known as snow blindness. So, you will need snow goggles to protect them. You might also need bottles of oxygen, which help you breathe and stop you from getting altitude sickness (see page 30).

Cross-country skis are great for moving fast across snowy landscapes.

WHO'S GOING WITH YOU?

Imagine you are going on an expedition to the mountains. Whom would you take as your traveling companions? Here are some ideas.

Expedition member: Tenzing Norgay (1914–1986)

Tenzing Norgay (on the right) was a Tibetan mountaineer who was the first person to reach the top of Mount Everest, along with New Zealand's Edmund Hillary. Tenzing started working on mountain expeditions by carrying equipment for other climbers. Climbing Everest made him world famous.

Potential job: Mountain guide

Expedition member: Kenton Cool (born 1973)

Kenton Cool is a British mountaineer. He has reached the summit of Everest an amazing 10 times and the summits of many more of the world's tallest mountains. He has even skied down Cho Oyu, the world's sixth-highest mountain! He is also one of the best mountain guides in the world.

Potential job: Expedition manager

Expedition member: Volcanologist

A volcanologist is a type of geologist who specializes in volcanoes. He or she could tell you about the features of the volcanoes you visit, such as craters and lava flows, and keep you safe on a volcano.

Potential job: Volcano guide

Expedition member: Geography teacher

Your geography teacher should know all about mountains! He or she will be able to tell you all about how mountains are made and point out all the different parts of mountains that you will see. Your teacher will also know about mountain people and the way they live.

Potential job: Expedition teacher

Expedition member: Wildlife expert

A wildlife expert could show you interesting plants and animals during your expeditions and tell you all about them (what they eat, how they live, and how they are adapted to mountains).

Potential job: Mountain wildlife expert

MOUNTAIN SURVIVAL

The hazards you will encounter when exploring mountaintops include severe weather, steep ground, slippery snow and ice, **avalanches**, and lightning. You need to protect yourself against hypothermia (getting extremely cold), frostbite, and dangerous falls. Never set out if the weather forecast is bad.

Amazing facts

During a thunderstorm, a summit is a dangerous place to be. Mountaineers have been killed by lightning in the past. Mountain storms can form quickly, and there is often nowhere to take shelter. Climbers and hikers are encouraged to climb during the morning, because there is far less chance of a storm coming before midday.

Altitude sickness

The higher you go on a mountain, the thinner the air gets, so there is less oxygen to breathe. At an altitude of about 10,000 feet (3,000 meters) or more, you start to notice that it gets harder to breathe. Many people begin to feel sick, have headaches, and feel weak. This is called acute mountain sickness or altitude sickness. This can go away after a day, but you might have to go back down the mountain to recover.

If something goes wrong...

Sometimes, no matter how careful people are, things go wrong in the mountains. People get injured, get sick, get stuck on cliffs, or get lost in bad weather. You can try to attract help with a flashlight or by blowing a whistle, or you can call a mountain rescue team by phone.

Don't forget

An emergency shelter will protect you from the wind and rain if you get stuck on a mountain. You could take a large waterproof bag to climb into, a small tent, or a group shelter, like a tent without poles, that three or four people can fit inside.

This mountaineer has dug a snow cave to use as a temporary shelter.

Crossing crevasses

A crevasse is a giant crack in a glacier, which can be more than about 100 feet (30 meters) deep. Never cross a glacier without an expert guide to show you a safe route, as crevasses can be hidden under thin layers of snow. Getting out of a crevasse is normally impossible without help and equipment such as harnesses and ropes.

These mountaineers are looking for a safe place to cross a glacier in the Karakoram Mountains of Pakistan.

Amazing facts

Avalanches move frighteningly fast. An avalanche of powdery snow falling down a steep slope travels at speeds of up to 155 miles (250 kilometers) per hour—as fast as a high-speed train. So, there is no way to outrun an avalanche.

Avalanches

An avalanche is a slide of snow down the side of a mountain. Avalanches are very dangerous to mountain explorers and **off-piste** skiers. They can sweep you downhill and then bury you under heavy snow. To avoid avalanches, read avalanche warnings and stay clear of mountain slopes where avalanches could strike. If you are unlucky enough to be caught in an avalanche, try swimming upward through the snow before it stops. If you get buried, try to make a space to breathe.

Don't forget

If there is a risk of avalanches where you are planning to go, you should take a radio locator beacon with you. That way, rescuers will be able to find you more quickly if you are buried. You could also carry an avalanche airbag. This will blow up like a balloon if you are knocked over by an avalanche and help to stop you from being buried.

Avalanches start when deep snow on a steep slope becomes unstable.

INTERVIEW WITH A MOUNTAIN EXPLORER

Neil Champion is a mountaineering and climbing instructor.

Q: When did you start exploring mountains?
A: I joined the Outdoors club at my high school when I was 13. Each year, we went on a field trip, where I was introduced to abseiling, climbing, hill walking, and wild camping. Great stuff!

Q: What do you like about exploring mountains?
A: Getting away from the crowds, being self-reliant, and the sheer fun and physical nature of mountaineering all attract me, as well as the wonderful landscapes you pass through.

Q: Do you have a favorite mountain?
A: I think the Cuillin of Skye, in Scotland, are my favorite. I have walked and climbed in them on a dozen or more different occasions and I still can't pretend to know them. They combine challenge, a fantastic landscape, and remoteness, all to the right degree.

Q: Is there a particular mountain you would like to climb?

A: Island Peak (at 20,300 feet, or almost 6,200 meters high) in Nepal. It's the mountain Edmund Hillary and Tenzing Norgay climbed in 1953 before they went on to conquer Everest. I'd like to succeed with that one.

Q: Do you have any mountaineering heroes?

A: Bill Tilman and Eric Shipton, two mountaineers who wandered in the Himalayas around 80 years ago and wrote some great accounts of their adventures.

Q: Have you ever gotten lost in the mountains?

A: Yes, lots of times! The important thing is not to panic and make a plan to relocate yourself using your map, compass, and memory of the ground you have just walked over.

Q: Is there anything that scares you about mountains?

A: Avalanches scare me. They don't respect age or climbing ability, and in spite of lots of scientific research into what causes them, they remain unpredictable. I almost got caught in one when ice climbing in the Alps. It frightened the life out of me!

Q: What's your favorite piece of clothing or equipment?

A: I think it has to be a headband. I use them all the time in the hills. They don't make your head boil like a wool hat can, but they keep your ears warm. I think the headband is an unsung hero.

CONSERVATION

Many of the world's mountain environments are threatened by human activities, even in the most remote places, where almost nobody lives. Our activities, such as mining and building dams, are affecting the animals, plants, and people that live on mountains, the people who live in mountains, and the landscape of the mountains themselves.

Tourism and leisure

More and more people are visiting and exploring mountains to enjoy their beauty, walk up them, climb on them, and for winter sports such as skiing and snowboarding. These people may leave pollution, erode the landscape, and use up precious resources such as water. But the development of tourist facilities, such as ski resorts, can bring jobs and income to local people.

As skiing becomes more popular, new ski resorts are built in the mountains.

Effects of global warming

Global warming is the gradual warming of the air in Earth's atmosphere, which most scientists agree is caused by activities such as burning fossil fuels and cutting down rain forests. In the mountains, the main effect of global warming is that glaciers are shrinking. In summer, melting glaciers are an important source of water for mountain animals, people, and crops. Water could be in short supply if glaciers melt completely.

Conservation

Building dams on mountain rivers means that valleys are flooded, along with the villages in them, and water supplies are often lost. Local people are often powerless to stop these developments. But they can protest against them, and sometimes they win the battle.

In 2012, villagers in the Lahaul Valley in northern India protested against the building of several large dams that would affect 26 villages.

The importance of mountains

Most people in the world do not live on mountains or even near mountains. They might not care about what happens to mountains, as long as they get the things they need from them, such as water, raw materials, and energy. But mountains are very important to the plants, animals, and people who live there and to the people who love to visit and explore them.

We need to take care of mountains in the same way that we need to take care of other parts of the world, such as rain forests and oceans. Damaging the mountains through mining, cutting down trees, building too many dams, and overusing the mountains for leisure will harm them and affect the lives of mountain people.

People find it rewarding to climb a mountain and to enjoy the view.

Exploring mountains can be an exciting and enjoyable experience.

Why visit the mountains?

Mountains are spectacular, awe-inspiring places to visit and explore. There are wild, remote, and beautiful places where people can escape to from their busy, everyday lives, perhaps catch a glimpse of a rare mountain animal, get to know how local people live and work, and try some exciting sports. There are still many mountains that nobody has visited and some summits that nobody has climbed. So, plan a trip, find some companions, get equipped, and get out and explore the mountains!

Don't forget

Take a camera to photograph the places you explore, the things you see, and the people you meet. There is a saying about exploring the world's wild places: "Take only photographs, leave only footprints." So, take as many photographs as you like, but take away your trash and leave everything exactly as you found it.

WORLD MOUNTAIN RANGES

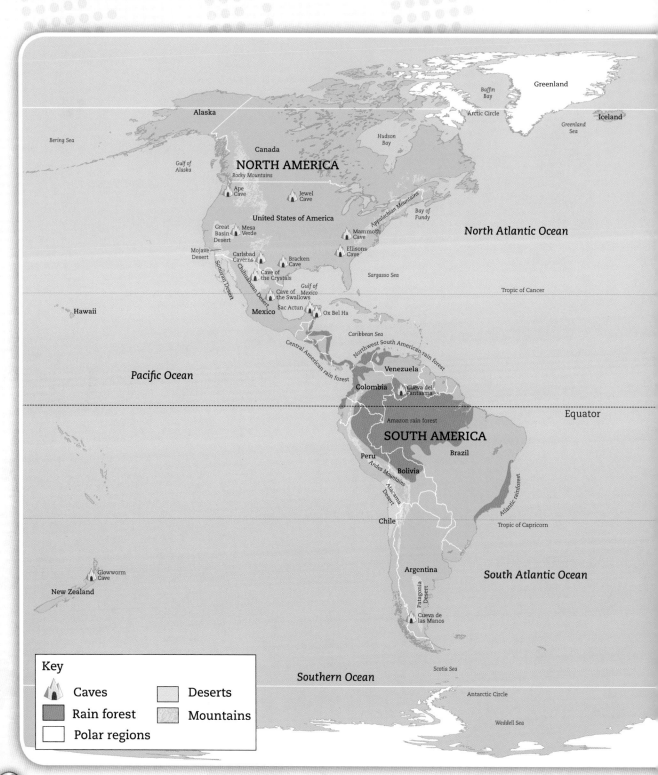

Greenland

Baffin Bay

Arctic Circle

Iceland

Greenland Sea

Alaska

Bering Sea

Hudson Bay

Gulf of Alaska

Canada

NORTH AMERICA
Rocky Mountains

Ape Cave

Jewel Cave

Appalachian Mountains

Bay of Fundy

North Atlantic Ocean

United States of America

Great Basin Desert

Mesa Verde

Mammoth Cave

Mojave Desert

Carlsbad Caverns

Bracken Cave

Ellisons Cave

Sonoran Desert

Chihuahuan Desert

Cave of the Crystals

Cave of the Swallows

Gulf of Mexico

Sargasso Sea

Tropic of Cancer

Hawaii

Sac Actun

Ox Bel Ha

Mexico

Caribbean Sea

Northwest South American rain forest

Central American rain forest

Pacific Ocean

Venezuela

Colombia

Cueva del Fantasma

Amazon rain forest

Equator

SOUTH AMERICA

Peru

Brazil

Andes Mountains

Bolivia

Atacama Desert

Atlantic rainforest

Chile

Tropic of Capricorn

Glowworm Cave

Argentina

South Atlantic Ocean

New Zealand

Patagonia Desert

Cueva de las Manos

Southern Ocean

Scotia Sea

Antarctic Circle

Weddell Sea

Key

- Caves
- Rain forest
- Polar regions
- Deserts
- Mountains

This map shows you where to find some of the world's mountains. There are many other exciting places to discover. Why not explore the oceans, caves, deserts, and rain forests on this map?

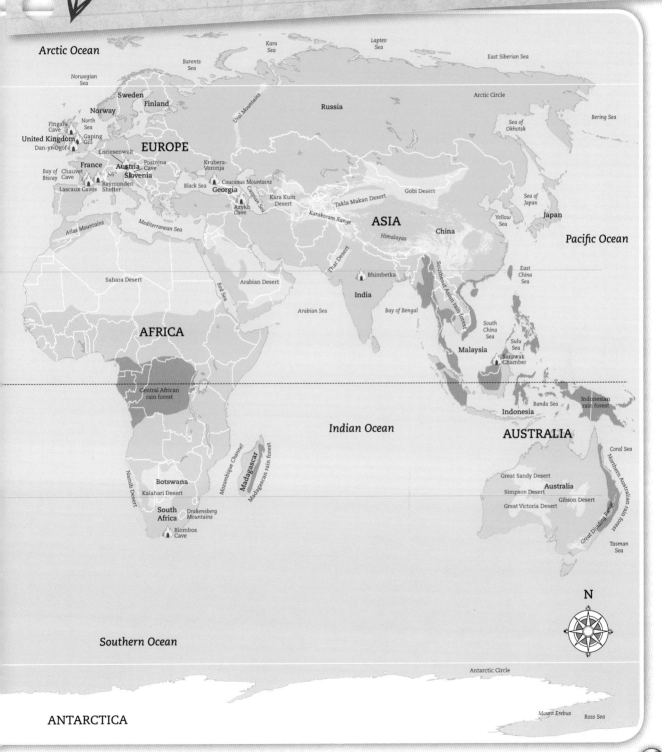

Arctic Ocean

Kara Sea

Barents Sea

Laptev Sea

East Siberian Sea

Norwegian Sea

Sweden

Finland

Norway

Russia

Arctic Circle

Sea of Okhotsk

Bering Sea

Fingal's Cave

North Sea

Gaping Gill

United Kingdom

Dan-yr-Ogof

EUROPE

Ural Mountains

Eisriesenwelt

France

Alps

Austria

Postojna Cave

Slovenia

Krubera-Voronja

Black Sea

Caucasus Mountains

Georgia

Kara Kum Desert

Takla Makan Desert

Gobi Desert

Sea of Japan

Yellow Sea

Japan

Pacific Ocean

Bay of Biscay

Chauvet Cave

Lascaux Caves

Raymonden Shelter

Azykh Cave

Caspian Sea

Karakoram Range

ASIA

Himalayas

China

Atlas Mountains

Mediterranean Sea

Thar Desert

Bhimbetka

East China Sea

Sahara Desert

Arabian Desert

Red Sea

India

Southeast Asian rain forest

South China Sea

Arabian Sea

Bay of Bengal

AFRICA

Central African rain forest

Sulu Sea

Malaysia

Sarawak Chamber

Indian Ocean

Banda Sea

Indonesian rain forest

Indonesia

AUSTRALIA

Coral Sea

Mozambique Channel

Madagascan rain forest

Madagascar

Great Sandy Desert

Australia

Simpson Desert

Gibson Desert

Great Victoria Desert

Northern Australian rain forest

Namib Desert

Botswana

Kalahari Desert

South Africa

Drakensberg Mountains

Great Dividing Range

Tasman Sea

Blombos Cave

N

Southern Ocean

Antarctic Circle

ANTARCTICA

Mount Erebus

Ross Sea

EXPLORER TRAVEL GUIDES

FACT FILE

THE HIGHEST MOUNTAINS

Mountain	Range	Height in feet (meters)
Everest	Himalayas	29,035 feet (8,850 meters)
K2	Karakoram	28,251 feet (8,611 meters)
Kangchenjunga	Himalayas	28,169 feet (8,586 meters)
Lhotse	Himalayas	27,890 feet (8,501 meters)
Makalu	Himalayas	27,766 feet (8,463 meters)
Cho Oyu	Himalayas	26,906 feet (8,201 meters)
Dhaulagiri	Himalayas	26,795 feet (8,167 meters)
Manaslu	Himalayas	26,781 feet (8,163 meters)
Nanga Parbat	Himalayas	26,660 feet (8,126 meters)
Annapurna	Himalayas	26,545 feet (8,091 meters)

THE HIGHEST MOUNTAINS BY CONTINENT

Continent	Mountain	Height in feet (meters)
Asia	Everest	29,035 feet (8,850 meters)
South America	Aconcagua	22,831 feet (6,959 meters)
North America	McKinley	20,322 feet (6,194 meters)
Africa	Kilimanjaro	19,341 feet (5,895 meters)
Europe	Elbrus	18,510 feet (5,642 meters)
Antarctica	Vinson Massif	16,050 feet (4,892 meters)
Australia	Kosciusko	7,310 feet (2,228 meters)

THE LONGEST MOUNTAIN RANGES

Range	Continent	Length in miles (kilometers)
The Andes	South America	4,500 miles (7,242 kilometers)
The Rockies	North America	3,750 miles (6,035 kilometers)
The Himalayas (including the Karakoram and Hindu Kush)	Asia	2,400 miles (3,862 kilometers)
The Great Dividing Range	Australia	2,250 miles (3,621 kilometers)
The Trans-Antarctic	Antarctica	2,200 miles (3,541 kilometers)

Historic first ascents

These are the people who were first to the top of some of the world's most famous mountains.

Mountain	Range	Climbers
Mont Blanc	Alps	Michel-Gabriel Paccard and his guide, Jacques Balmat (Sardinia), 1786
Eiger	Alps	Charles Barrington and guides (United Kingdom, Switzerland), 1858
Matterhorn	Alps	Edward Whymper (United Kingdom) and others, 1865
McKinley	Alaska Range	Hudson Stuck and others (United States), 1913
Annapurna	Himalayas	Maurice Herzog and Louis Lachenal (France), 1950
Everest	Himalayas	Tenzing Norgay (Nepal) and Edmund Hillary (New Zealand), 1953
K2	Karakoram	Achille Compagnoni and Lino Lacedelli (Italy), 1954

Underwater mountains

- Mountains under the oceans (called seamounts) dwarf the mountains on dry land! They form where magma leaks out from under Earth's crust onto the ocean floor, so they are really underwater volcanoes.
- The highest seamount is Mauna Loa, at 33,465 feet (10,200 meters). Its top forms part of the island of Hawaii.
- The longest mountain range is the mid-ocean ridge, which stretches about 40,000 miles (65,000 kilometers) around Earth, under the Atlantic and Pacific Oceans.

GLOSSARY

active volcano volcano that is erupting or that has recently erupted and may erupt again soon

adapted describes a plant or animal that has features that allow it to live in its habitat

alpine relating to high mountains

altitude how high above the level of the sea something is

altitude sickness medical problem that happens because of the lack of oxygen at very high altitudes. People need oxygen to breathe.

ash tiny particles of rock formed when magma is blasted into tiny pieces as it leaves a volcano, cools, and becomes solid

avalanche slide of snow down the side of a mountain

biome community of plants and animals that live in a very large habitat, such as a mountain range

climate pattern of weather that happens in a place over a long time

coniferous tree with leaves like needles that do not fall off in the fall, and that grows cones

crevasse deep crack in a glacier

crust solid, rocky skin of Earth that makes up the surface we stand on

deciduous describes a tree that loses its leaves in the fall and gets new leaves in the spring

deforestation cutting down the trees in a forest, leaving bare ground where trees cannot grow again

erosion process that wears away rocks and breaks down mountains

extinct describes a volcano that is dead. It will never erupt again.

face sloping side of a mountain

foothill hill between a high mountain range and the plains below

glacier slow-moving river of ice that flows down from a mountain, gouging out rock as it moves

GPS (global positioning system) receiver electronic gadget that detects signals from satellites in space and uses them to calculate its exact position on Earth's surface

hibernate go into a deep sleep during the winter to use as little energy as possible

indigenous people who originated in the place they now live

lava molten rock when it comes out of a volcano and flows across the surface. Lava turns to rock when it cools down.

magma molten rock under or in Earth's crust

mountain range collection of mountains in the same area of the world, such as the Himalayas or the Andes

nomad person who regularly moves from place to place instead of having a permanent home

off-piste away from prepared ski runs; also called backcountry

pack animal animal that carries loads from place to place

pass gap or low point in a mountain range that people use to get from one side of the range to the other

pumice type of rock sometimes formed when a volcano erupts. It contains so many air bubbles that it floats.

pyroclastic flow roasting hot mixture of rock, ash, and gas that flows at high speed down the side of a volcano

ridge long, narrow mountain range

saddle lower part of a ridge between two higher points

species type of animal

summit highest part of a mountain. Some mountains have two or more high parts, which are all known as summits.

tectonic plate one of the giant pieces that form Earth's crust

tundra land in the Arctic that has soil that is always frozen under the surface

volcano place where magma from beneath Earth's crust comes out onto the surface, often building up a mountain

volcanologist person who studies volcanoes

FIND OUT MORE

Books

Green, Jen. *Mountains (Geography Wise)*. New York: PowerKids, 2011.

Macleod, Alasdair. *Explorers: Great Tales of Adventure and Endurance*. New York: Dorling Kindersley, 2010.

Waldron, Melanie. *Mountains (Habitat Survival)*. Chicago: Raintree, 2013.

Web sites

education.nationalgeographic.com/education/topics/mountains/?ar_a=1
Click on the entries on this National Geographic page to learn more about a variety of topics connected to mountains.

www.evk2cnr.org/WebCams/PyramidOne/everest-webcam.html
This webcam shows live pictures of Mount Everest!

www.theuiaa.org
The web site of the International Mountaineering and Climbing Federation tells you everything you need to know about mountain climbing and expeditions, including information for young people.

video.nationalgeographic.com/video/places/parks-and-nature-places/mountains-volcanoes
This National Geographic web site has some amazing videos of mountains and volcanoes.

volcanoes.usgs.gov
The volcano hazards section of the U.S. Geological Survey site has links to webcams on some active volcanoes.

Places to visit

American Museum of Natural History
Central Park West at 79th Street
New York, N.Y. 10024-5192
www.amnh.org

Denali National Park and Preserve
Denali Park, Alaska 99755-0009
www.nps.gov/dena
This national park features the highest summit in the United States—
Mount McKinley, which is 20,320 feet (6,194 meters) above sea level.

Mount Rainier National Park
Ashford, Washington 98304
www.nps.gov/mora
This national park includes Mount Rainier, a huge stratovolcano.

Rocky Mountain National Park
Estes Park, Colorado 80517-8397
www.nps.gov/romo
This national park lets you experience the Rocky Mountain mountain
range up close and also see a wide variety of wildlife.

Further research

Look back over the topics you have read about in the book. Which
topics did you enjoy most? Perhaps it was how mountains are made,
volcanoes, mountain climbing, or mountain animals? Try researching
your favorite topic in more detail by visiting the web sites listed on
these pages and others and by visiting your local library.

INDEX